For Alex and Patrick

KEEP CALM AND CARRY ON

GOOD ADVICE FOR HARD TIMES

EBURY
PRESS

1

First published in 2009 by Ebury Press, an imprint of Ebury Publishing
20 Vauxhall Bridge Road, SW1V 2SA

This edition published in 2022

Ebury Press is part of the Penguin Random House group of companies
whose addresses can be found at global.penguinrandomhouse.com

www.penguin.co.uk

A CIP catalogue record for this book is available from the British Library

ISBN 9780091933715

Printed and bound in Great Britain by Clays Ltd, Elcograf S.p.A.

The authorised representative in the EEA is Penguin Random House
Ireland, Morrison Chambers, 32 Nassau Street, Dublin D02 YH68

MIX
Paper from
responsible sources
FSC® C018179

WISE MEN DON'T NEED ADVICE. FOOLS WON'T TAKE IT.

Benjamin Franklin

CONTENTS

INTRODUCTION

Keep Calm and Carry On. The British have never been terribly good at the more touchy-feely aspects of self-help and inspiration – the kind peddled so effectively in the United States for decades and now beloved in the rest of the modern world. When the British have been stuck in a spot of bother in the past, such as the odd World War, we have tended to resort to more formal and restrained modes of address – 'pull yourself together', 'stiff upper lip and all that, old man'. This is the very world that spawned Keep Calm and Carry On.

It was one of three posters produced by the British Government's Ministry of Information on the eve of war in 1939. The other two were 'Freedom is in Peril' and 'Your Courage, Your Cheerfulness, Your Resolution Will Bring Us Victory'. Simple reassuring instructions, each topped with the commanding seal of King George VI's crown. Two and a half million copies of the Keep Calm and Carry On sheets were printed, but they would be distributed only in the imminent threat of a German invasion. Thankfully they never saw the light of day and were almost all pulped. So that might have been that, if one of the few remaining posters hadn't been discovered in a dusty box of old books bought at auction by Northumbrian bookseller Stuart Manley.

Though they didn't initially know what the poster was, Mr Manley and his wife liked it so much they framed it and hung it in their bookshop. They weren't the only ones who found its stark, simple reassurance engaging. In fact they had so many enquiries about it from customers that in the end they decided to have some copies printed. It seemed that in the seventy years since its first appearance, its very British soothing strength hadn't lost any of its appeal. The bookshop has gone on to sell tens of thousands of the poster, not to mention mugs, T-shirts and tea towels, with customers including everyone from *Top Gear* presenters to Buckingham Palace and Downing Street. Its message, it seemed, was just as effective a tonic for those labouring under modern anxieties as those who endured the Blitz. But it wasn't until the uncharted waters of the economic downturn began to rise that the mantra really came into its own. Since the autumn of 2008 it has quite literally become the pin-up of our current predicament, with even the BBC posing the question: is this the greatest motivational poster ever?

So what you hold in your hand is the book of the poster – a modest attempt at inspiration for hard times: a restorative mixture of advice, entertainment and inspiration to help you through. In an age not just of recession but also information overload, you need a source of wisdom that doesn't hang about or mince its words, so these quotes have been chosen not only for their ability to echo the universal good sense of the original poster but also to echo the virtue of its brevity. Drawing on over two millennia of common sense from home and abroad, from Cicero to Churchill, *Keep Calm and Carry On* attempts to put its finger on the mess we are in and, moving forward from that sorry mess, what can make life truly worthwhile.

Enjoy – and pass on the good cheer.

With thanks to Barter Books
Home of the original WWII poster
www.barterbooks.co.uk

KEEP
CALM

CRISIS

WHAT WE ANTICIPATE SELDOM OCCURS; WHAT WE LEAST EXPECT GENERALLY HAPPENS.

Benjamin Disraeli

CALAMITY *n.*
A MORE THAN
COMMONLY PLAIN
AND UNMISTAKABLE
REMINDER THAT THE
AFFAIRS OF THIS LIFE
ARE NOT OF OUR
OWN ORDERING.

Ambrose Bierce

IF YOU CAN KEEP
YOUR HEAD WHEN
ALL ABOUT YOU ARE
LOSING THEIRS, IT'S
JUST POSSIBLE YOU
HAVEN'T GRASPED
THE SITUATION.

Jean Kerr

IT ISN'T SO MUCH THAT HARD TIMES ARE COMING; THE CHANGE OBSERVED IS MOSTLY SOFT TIMES GOING.

Groucho Marx

HE WHO THINKS HE IS RAISING A MOUND MAY ONLY IN REALITY BE DIGGING A PIT.

Ernest Bramah

THE
ECONOMY

ECONOMIC ADVANCE IS NOT THE SAME THING AS HUMAN PROGRESS.

John Clapham

IT'S A RECESSION WHEN YOUR NEIGHBOR LOSES HIS JOB; IT'S A DEPRESSION WHEN YOU LOSE YOURS.

Harry S Truman

BLESSED ARE THE YOUNG, FOR THEY SHALL INHERIT THE NATIONAL DEBT.

Herbert Hoover

THE MEEK SHALL INHERIT THE EARTH, BUT NOT ITS MINERAL RIGHTS.

J Paul Getty

ECONOMISTS

AN ECONOMIST IS AN EXPERT WHO WILL KNOW TOMORROW WHY THE THINGS HE PREDICTED YESTERDAY DIDN'T HAPPEN TODAY.

Laurence J Peter

IF ALL ECONOMISTS WERE LAID END TO END, THEY WOULD NOT REACH A CONCLUSION.

George Bernard Shaw

THE ONLY FUNCTION OF ECONOMIC FORECASTING IS TO MAKE ASTROLOGY LOOK RESPECTABLE.

John Kenneth Galbraith

SPECULATION

PREDICTION IS VERY DIFFICULT, ESPECIALLY ABOUT THE FUTURE.

Niels Bohr

I CAN CALCULATE THE MOTION OF HEAVENLY BODIES, BUT NOT THE MADNESS OF PEOPLE.

Sir Isaac Newton, after losing a fortune in the 1720 South Sea Bubble

OCTOBER: THIS IS ONE OF THE PECULIARLY DANGEROUS MONTHS TO SPECULATE IN STOCKS. THE OTHERS ARE JULY, JANUARY, SEPTEMBER, APRIL, NOVEMBER, MAY, MARCH, JUNE, DECEMBER, AUGUST AND FEBRUARY.

Mark Twain

IT IS UNFORTUNATE
WE CAN'T BUY
MANY BUSINESS
EXECUTIVES FOR
WHAT THEY ARE
WORTH AND SELL
THEM FOR WHAT
THEY THINK THEY
ARE WORTH.

Malcolm Forbes

THE SAFE WAY
TO DOUBLE YOUR
MONEY IS TO FOLD IT
OVER ONCE AND PUT
IT IN YOUR POCKET.

Frank Hubbard

THE GREAT
CRASH OF
1929

I CANNOT HELP BUT RAISE A DISSENTING VOICE TO STATEMENTS THAT WE ARE LIVING IN A FOOL'S PARADISE, AND THAT PROSPERITY IN THIS COUNTRY MUST NECESSARILY DIMINISH AND RECEDE IN THE NEAR FUTURE.

*E H H Simmons, President,
New York Stock Exchange, 12 January 1928*

**STOCK PRICES
HAVE REACHED
WHAT LOOKS LIKE
A PERMANENTLY
HIGH PLATEAU.**

Irving Fisher, economist, 17 October 1929

THIS CRASH IS NOT GOING TO HAVE MUCH EFFECT ON BUSINESS.

Arthur Reynolds, Chairman of Continental Illinois Bank of Chicago, 24 October 1929

WHILE THE CRASH ONLY TOOK PLACE SIX MONTHS AGO, I AM CONVINCED WE HAVE NOW PASSED THE WORST AND WITH CONTINUED UNITY OF EFFORT WE SHALL RAPIDLY RECOVER.

Herbert Hoover, 1 May 1930

THE CRUNCH

WE WILL NEVER RETURN TO THE OLD BOOM AND BUST.

Gordon Brown, Budget Statement, 2007

HE IS LIKE SOME SHERRY-CRAZED OLD DOWAGER WHO HAS LOST THE FAMILY SILVER AT ROULETTE, AND WHO NOW DECIDES TO DOUBLE UP BY BETTING THE HOUSE AS WELL.

Boris Johnson on Gordon Brown

ONE OF THE VERY DIFFICULT PARTS OF THE DECISION I MADE ON THE FINANCIAL CRISIS WAS TO USE HARD-WORKING PEOPLE'S MONEY TO HELP PREVENT THERE TO BE A CRISIS.

George W Bush, 2009

YOUR COMPANY IS NOW BANKRUPT, AND OUR COUNTRY IS IN A STATE OF CRISIS, BUT YOU GET TO KEEP $480 MILLION. I HAVE A VERY BASIC QUESTION: IS THAT FAIR?

Henry Waxman, questioning Lehman Brothers CEO Richard Fuld

IT'S ALMOST LIKE SEEING A GUY SHOW UP AT THE SOUP KITCHEN IN HIGH HAT AND TUXEDO. IT KIND OF MAKES YOU A LITTLE BIT SUSPICIOUS.

Congressman Gary Ackerman after Chrysler, Ford and General Motors executives went to Washington to ask for $25 billion in loans – arriving in their private jets

BIG
BUSINESS

BEHIND EVERY GREAT FORTUNE THERE IS A CRIME.

Honoré de Balzac

HELL, THERE ARE NO RULES HERE – WE'RE TRYING TO ACCOMPLISH SOMETHING.

Thomas A Edison

IF YOU CAN BUILD A BUSINESS UP BIG ENOUGH, IT'S RESPECTABLE.

Will Rogers

BUSINESS IS THE ART OF EXTRACTING MONEY FROM ANOTHER MAN'S POCKET WITHOUT RESORTING TO VIOLENCE.

Max Amsterdam

CORPORATION *n*: AN INGENIOUS DEVICE FOR OBTAINING INDIVIDUAL PROFIT WITHOUT INDIVIDUAL RESPONSIBILITY.

Ambrose Bierce

**YOU CAN FOOL
ALL THE PEOPLE
ALL THE TIME IF THE
ADVERTISING IS
RIGHT AND THE
BUDGET IS BIG
ENOUGH.**

Joseph E Levine

CATCH A MAN A
FISH, AND YOU CAN
SELL IT TO HIM.
TEACH A MAN TO
FISH, AND YOU RUIN
A WONDERFUL
BUSINESS
OPPORTUNITY.

Karl Marx

BANKING

A BANKER IS A FELLOW WHO LENDS YOU HIS UMBRELLA WHEN THE SUN IS SHINING, BUT WANTS IT BACK THE MINUTE IT BEGINS TO RAIN.

Mark Twain

I BELIEVE THAT BANKING INSTITUTIONS ARE MORE DANGEROUS TO OUR LIBERTIES THAN STANDING ARMIES.

Thomas Jefferson

A BANK IS A PLACE THAT WILL LEND YOU MONEY IF YOU CAN PROVE THAT YOU DON'T NEED IT.

Bob Hope

MONEY

MONEY OFTEN
COSTS TOO MUCH.

Ralph Waldo Emerson

EXPENDITURES RISE
TO MEET INCOME.

Parkinson's Second Law

MAKE MONEY YOUR GOD AND IT WILL PLAGUE YOU LIKE THE DEVIL.

Henry Fielding

**ACQUAINTANCE *n*:
A PERSON WHOM WE
KNOW WELL ENOUGH
TO BORROW FROM,
BUT NOT WELL
ENOUGH TO LEND TO.**

Ambrose Bierce

CREDIT IS A SYSTEM WHEREBY A PERSON WHO CAN NOT PAY GETS ANOTHER PERSON WHO CAN NOT PAY TO GUARANTEE THAT HE CAN PAY.

Charles Dickens

TODAY, THERE ARE THREE KINDS OF PEOPLE: THE HAVE'S, THE HAVE-NOT'S, AND THE HAVE-NOT-PAID-FOR-WHAT-THEY-HAVE'S.

Earl Wilson

WEALTH – ANY INCOME THAT IS AT LEAST ONE HUNDRED DOLLARS MORE A YEAR THAN THE INCOME OF ONE'S WIFE'S SISTER'S HUSBAND.

H L Mencken

ANNUAL INCOME TWENTY POUNDS, ANNUAL EXPENDITURE NINETEEN NINETEEN AND SIX, RESULT HAPPINESS. ANNUAL INCOME TWENTY POUNDS, ANNUAL EXPENDITURE TWENTY POUNDS OUGHT AND SIX, RESULT MISERY.

Mr Micawber, David Copperfield

LET US ALL BE HAPPY, AND LIVE WITHIN OUR MEANS, EVEN IF WE HAVE TO BORROW THE MONEY TO DO IT WITH.

Artemus Ward

DEBT

BORROWED MONEY
SHORTENS TIME.

Chinese proverb

CREDITORS HAVE BETTER MEMORIES THAN DEBTORS.

Benjamin Franklin

ARMAMENTS, UNIVERSAL DEBT AND PLANNED OBSOLESCENCE – THOSE ARE THE THREE PILLARS OF WESTERN PROSPERITY.

Aldous Huxley

BEWARE OF LITTLE EXPENSES; A SMALL LEAK WILL SINK A GREAT SHIP.

Benjamin Franklin

I'M LIVING SO FAR BEYOND MY INCOME THAT WE MAY ALMOST BE SAID TO BE LIVING APART.

e e cummings

RISK

**IT AIN'T WHAT YOU
DON'T KNOW THAT
GETS YOU INTO
TROUBLE. IT'S WHAT
YOU KNOW FOR SURE
THAT JUST AIN'T SO.**

Mark Twain

BETTER BREAD WITH WATER THAN CAKE WITH TROUBLE.

Russian Proverb

GREED

LUXURY: THE LUST FOR COMFORT, THAT STEALTHY THING THAT ENTERS THE HOUSE AS A GUEST, AND THEN BECOMES A HOST, AND THEN A MASTER.

Kahlil Gibran

THE DARKEST HOUR IN ANY MAN'S LIFE IS WHEN HE SITS DOWN TO PLAN HOW TO GET MONEY WITHOUT EARNING IT.

Horace Greeley

FOR A GREEDY MAN
EVEN HIS TOMB IS
TOO SMALL.

Tajikistani Proverb

WORK

BEWARE THE BARRENNESS OF A BUSY LIFE.

Socrates

THE MAJORITY OF ENGLISHMEN AND AMERICANS HAVE NO LIFE BUT IN THEIR WORK.

John Stuart Mill

WORK EXPANDS SO AS TO FILL THE TIME AVAILABLE FOR ITS COMPLETION.

Parkinson's First Law

WORK IS GOOD PROVIDED YOU DO NOT FORGET TO LIVE.

Bantu Proverb

WE MAKE A LIVING BY WHAT WE GET, BUT WE MAKE A LIFE BY WHAT WE GIVE.

Winston Churchill

CARRY ON

STRENGTH IN ADVERSITY

THERE IS NO EDUCATION LIKE ADVERSITY.

Benjamin Disraeli

**ADVERSITY HAS THE
EFFECT OF ELICITING
TALENTS WHICH,
IN PROSPEROUS
CIRCUMSTANCES,
WOULD HAVE LAIN
DORMANT.**

Horace

WHEN WRITTEN IN CHINESE THE WORD 'CRISIS' IS COMPOSED OF TWO CHARACTERS – ONE REPRESENTS DANGER AND THE OTHER REPRESENTS OPPORTUNITY.

John F Kennedy

IN THE MIDST OF WINTER, I FOUND THERE WAS, WITHIN ME, AN INVINCIBLE SUMMER.

Albert Camus

MISTAKES
AND
FAILURES

A LIFE SPENT MAKING MISTAKES IS NOT ONLY MORE HONOURABLE BUT MORE USEFUL THAN A LIFE SPENT DOING NOTHING.

George Bernard Shaw

SUCCESS IS THE ABILITY TO GO FROM ONE FAILURE TO ANOTHER WITH NO LOSS OF ENTHUSIASM.

Winston Churchill

FAILURES ARE FINGER POSTS ON THE ROAD TO ACHIEVEMENT.

C S Lewis

THE GREATEST MISTAKE A MAN CAN EVER MAKE IS TO BE AFRAID OF MAKING ONE.

Elbert Hubbard

THE
GOOD
LIFE

THERE IS MORE
TO LIFE THAN
INCREASING
ITS SPEED.

Mahatma Gandhi

OUR LIFE IS FRITTERED AWAY BY DETAIL. SIMPLIFY, SIMPLIFY.

Henry David Thoreau

IF YOU CAN SPEND
A PERFECTLY
USELESS AFTERNOON
IN A PERFECTLY
USELESS MANNER,
YOU HAVE LEARNED
HOW TO LIVE.

Lin Yutang

USE YOUR HEALTH, EVEN TO THE POINT OF WEARING IT OUT. THAT IS WHAT IT IS FOR. SPEND ALL YOU HAVE BEFORE YOU DIE; DO NOT OUTLIVE YOURSELF.

George Bernard Shaw

THE BEST PORTION
OF A GOOD MAN'S
LIFE – HIS LITTLE,
NAMELESS,
UNREMEMBERED
ACTS OF KINDNESS.

William Wordsworth

ALWAYS BE KIND, FOR EVERYONE IS FIGHTING A HARD BATTLE.

Plato

HAPPINESS

HAPPINESS DEPENDS
UPON OURSELVES.

Aristotle

TO BE WITHOUT SOME OF THE THINGS YOU WANT IS AN INDISPENSABLE PART OF HAPPINESS.

Bertrand Russell

THE FOOLISH MAN SEEKS HAPPINESS IN THE DISTANCE, THE WISE GROWS IT UNDER HIS FEET.

James Oppenheim

HAPPINESS IS NOTHING MORE THAN GOOD HEALTH AND A BAD MEMORY.

Albert Schweitzer

NOW AND THEN IT'S GOOD TO PAUSE IN OUR PURSUIT OF HAPPINESS AND JUST BE HAPPY.

Guillaume Apollinaire

WE DEEM THOSE HAPPY WHO FROM THE EXPERIENCE OF LIFE HAVE LEARNED TO BEAR ITS ILLS, WITHOUT BEING OVERCOME BY THEM.

Juvenal

**TO BE HAPPY FOR AN
HOUR, GET DRUNK;
TO BE HAPPY FOR A
YEAR, FALL IN LOVE;
TO BE HAPPY FOR
LIFE, TAKE UP
GARDENING.**

Chinese proverb

A LIFETIME OF HAPPINESS! NO MAN ALIVE COULD BEAR IT: IT WOULD BE HELL ON EARTH.

George Bernard Shaw

A GOOD
WALK

A VIGOROUS FIVE-MILE WALK WILL DO MORE GOOD FOR AN UNHAPPY BUT OTHERWISE HEALTHY ADULT THAN ALL THE MEDICINE AND PSYCHOLOGY IN THE WORLD.

Paul Dudley White

AFTER A DAY'S WALK EVERYTHING HAS TWICE ITS USUAL VALUE.

G M Trevelyan

**THE BEST REMEDY
FOR THOSE WHO ARE
AFRAID, LONELY OR
UNHAPPY IS TO GO
OUTSIDE, SOMEWHERE
WHERE THEY CAN BE
QUIET, ALONE WITH THE
HEAVENS, NATURE AND
GOD. BECAUSE ONLY
THEN DOES ONE FEEL
THAT ALL IS AS
IT SHOULD BE.**

Anne Frank

FRIENDSHIP

OF ALL THE THINGS THAT WISDOM PROVIDES TO HELP ONE LIVE ONE'S ENTIRE LIFE IN HAPPINESS, THE GREATEST BY FAR IS THE POSSESSION OF FRIENDSHIP. EATING OR DRINKING WITHOUT A FRIEND IS THE LIFE OF A LION OR A WOLF.

Epicurus

YOU CAN MAKE MORE FRIENDS IN TWO MONTHS BY BECOMING INTERESTED IN OTHER PEOPLE THAN YOU CAN IN TWO YEARS BY TRYING TO GET PEOPLE INTERESTED IN YOU.

Dale Carnegie

THRIFT

THERE ARE PLENTY OF WAYS TO GET AHEAD. THE FIRST IS SO BASIC I'M ALMOST EMBARRASSED TO SAY IT: SPEND LESS THAN YOU EARN.

Paul Clitheroe

WE MUST BEWARE OF TRYING TO BUILD A SOCIETY IN WHICH NOBODY COUNTS FOR ANYTHING EXCEPT A POLITICIAN OR AN OFFICIAL, A SOCIETY WHERE ENTERPRISE GAINS NO REWARD AND THRIFT NO PRIVILEGES.

Winston Churchill

**DON'T JUDGE
EACH DAY BY THE
HARVEST YOU REAP,
BUT BY THE SEEDS
THAT YOU PLANT.**

Robert Louis Stevenson

I BELIEVE THAT THRIFT IS ESSENTIAL TO WELL-ORDERED LIVING.

John D Rockefeller

CANNOT PEOPLE
REALIZE HOW
LARGE AN INCOME
IS THRIFT?

Cicero

DON'T
WORRY

I AM AN OPTIMIST.
IT DOESN'T SEEM
TOO MUCH USE
BEING ANYTHING
ELSE.

Winston Churchill

**WORRY OFTEN
GIVES A SMALL
THING A BIG
SHADOW.**

Swedish proverb

IF YOU CAN'T SLEEP, THEN GET UP AND DO SOMETHING INSTEAD OF LYING THERE AND WORRYING. IT'S THE WORRY THAT GETS YOU, NOT THE LOSS OF SLEEP.

Dale Carnegie

**A WORRIED MAN
COULD BORROW A
LOT OF TROUBLE
WITH PRACTICALLY
NO COLLATERAL.**

Helen Nielsen

DON'T WORRY ABOUT THE WORLD COMING TO AN END TODAY. IT'S ALREADY TOMORROW IN AUSTRALIA.

Charles M Schulz

HURRYING AND WORRYING ARE NOT THE SAME AS STRENGTH.

Nigerian proverb

IT AIN'T NO USE
PUTTING UP YOUR
UMBRELLA TILL
IT RAINS.

Alice Caldwell Rice

COPING

THE BEST WAY OUT IS ALWAYS THROUGH.

Robert Frost

IT IS A COMMON
EXPERIENCE
THAT A PROBLEM
DIFFICULT AT NIGHT
IS RESOLVED IN THE
MORNING AFTER THE
COMMITTEE OF SLEEP
HAS WORKED ON IT.

John Steinbeck

ALWAYS LAUGH WHEN YOU CAN. IT IS CHEAP MEDICINE.

Lord Byron

THE ROBBED THAT SMILES, STEALS SOMETHING FROM THE THIEF.

William Shakespeare

HE WHO HAS A WHY TO LIVE CAN BEAR ALMOST ANY HOW.

Friedrich Nietzsche

I CAN IMAGINE NO
MORE COMFORTABLE
FRAME OF MIND FOR
THE CONDUCT OF
LIFE THAN A
HUMOROUS
RESIGNATION.

W Somerset Maugham

THE ART OF
LIVING LIES LESS
IN ELIMINATING
OUR TROUBLES
THAN IN GROWING
WITH THEM.

Bernard M Baruch

WHILE THERE IS A
CHANCE OF THE WORLD
GETTING THROUGH ITS
TROUBLES, I HOLD THAT
A REASONABLE MAN
HAS TO BEHAVE AS
THOUGH HE WERE SURE
OF IT. IF AT THE END
YOUR CHEERFULNESS IS
NOT JUSTIFIED, AT ANY
RATE YOU WILL HAVE
BEEN CHEERFUL.

H G Wells

LIFE IS A SHIPWRECK, BUT WE MUST NOT FORGET TO SING IN THE LIFEBOATS.

Voltaire

IF ALL MISFORTUNES
WERE LAID IN ONE
COMMON HEAP
WHENCE EVERYONE
MUST TAKE AN
EQUAL PORTION,
MOST PEOPLE
WOULD BE
CONTENTED TO
TAKE THEIR OWN
AND DEPART.

Socrates

MY RELIGION OF LIFE IS ALWAYS TO BE CHEERFUL.

George Meredith

THERE IS NO TROUBLE SO GREAT OR GRAVE THAT CANNOT BE MUCH DIMINISHED BY A NICE CUP OF TEA.

Bernard-Paul Heroux

CONSOLATION

HOW CAN THEY SAY MY LIFE IS NOT A SUCCESS? HAVE I NOT FOR MORE THAN 60 YEARS GOT ENOUGH TO EAT AND ESCAPED BEING EATEN?

Logan Pearsall Smith

IF WE WILL BE QUIET AND READY ENOUGH, WE SHALL FIND COMPENSATION IN EVERY DISAPPOINTMENT.

Henry David Thoreau

PROSPERITY IS NOT WITHOUT MANY FEARS AND DISTASTES, AND ADVERSITY IS NOT WITHOUT COMFORTS AND HOPES.

Francis Bacon

**MY LIFE HAS
BEEN FILLED
WITH TERRIBLE
MISFORTUNE; MOST
OF WHICH NEVER
HAPPENED.**

Michel de Montaigne

CHANGE

TWENTY YEARS FROM NOW YOU WILL BE MORE DISAPPOINTED BY THE THINGS THAT YOU DIDN'T DO THAN BY THE ONES YOU DID DO. SO THROW OFF THE BOWLINES. SAIL AWAY FROM SAFE HARBOR. CATCH THE TRADE WINDS IN YOUR SAILS. EXPLORE. DREAM. DISCOVER.

Mark Twain

THE ONLY DIFFERENCE BETWEEN A RUT AND A GRAVE IS THEIR DIMENSIONS.

Ellen Glasgow

**IF YOU'RE IN A
BAD SITUATION,
DON'T WORRY
IT'LL CHANGE. IF
YOU'RE IN A GOOD
SITUATION, DON'T
WORRY IT'LL
CHANGE.**

John A Simone Sr

IF AT FIRST YOU DON'T SUCCEED, TRY, TRY AGAIN. THEN QUIT. THERE'S NO POINT IN BEING A DAMN FOOL ABOUT IT.

W C Fields